WRONGFUL TERMINATION IN DELAWARE

A Survival Guide
For True Employees Fired for False Reasons

John M. LaRosa, Esq.

Jacobs & Whitehall
21750 Hardy Oak Blvd
Suite 104
#51700
San Antonio, Texas 78258
www.jacobsandwhitehall.com

Ordering Information:

Quantity sales. Special discounts are available on quantity purchases by corporations, associations, and others. For details, contact the publisher at the address above.

Orders by U.S. trade bookstores and wholesalers. Please contact Jacobs & Whitehall: Tel: (888) 991-2766 or visit www.jacobsandwhitehall.com.

Printed in the United States of America

Published in 2022

ISBN: 978-1-954506-40-4

PREFACE

For more than two decades now, I have devoted my career to representing employees in Delaware, Pennsylvania, and New Jersey in cases involving wrongful termination of employment or other unlawful employment actions, including denial of promotion, denial of hire, and harassment based on discrimination, retaliation, or other illegal reasons. I have been fortunate to help hundreds of former, current, and potential employees in my many years of practice as an employee rights attorney.

But for each potential client who calls my office, I suspect there are many more employees who suffer in silence, wondering whether their legal rights have been violated by their employer and whether they have experienced an issue with which an employee rights attorney could help. These employees may hesitate to contact a lawyer about a potential violation of their employment law rights. To make matters worse, there are very few books aimed at explaining to these employees their rights and responsibilities with respect to their employers. There are even fewer books specifically intended to explain, for employees *who work within the State of Delaware*, their rights with regard to their companies. With this book, I aim to do just that.

Most books about employment law are treatises written for employers, employment and labor lawyers, or law school students. Further, most treatises about employment law are filled with footnotes and case citations that are understandable mainly to attorneys and to law professors. This is not such a book or treatise.

Instead, this book was written with employees in mind. The readers for whom I intend this book are laypeople (non-lawyers) who work in the First State. This book is for any employee of a private or a public employer in Delaware who believes their employment has been wrongfully terminated or that their employment rights have been violated by their employer.

The purpose of this book is to provide the reader with an understanding of employee rights in Delaware - particularly with respect to wrongful termination - as well as a general understanding of what an employment lawyer does, which includes looking at *why* an action really was taken against an employee as much as *what* action was taken against the employee. For those who are wondering if their employment was wrongfully terminated or if they have another employment issue that merits contacting an employment attorney, I hope this book will be informative and helpful. Furthermore, if you are one of those individuals unsure whether you should seek an attorney, this book might even answer the often-posed question: "Do I have a case?"

DEDICATION

I dedicate this book to the memory of my parents, Frank and Lillian LaRosa, who taught me the value of hard work at a young age which has served me well in my life's work as an employee rights lawyer. I also dedicate this book to my mentor, Thomas S. Neuberger, Esquire, who taught me how to advocate for employees and other individuals in a society that often favors corporations and institutional wealth and power over human beings and their inalienable civil rights. Finally, I dedicate this book to my loving wife and our inquisitive daughter. I strive to make all of them proud.

Disclaimer

This publication is intended to be used for educational purposes only. No legal advice is being given, and no attorney-client relationship is intended to be created by reading this material. The author assumes no liability for any errors or omissions or for how this book or its contents are used or interpreted, or for any consequences resulting directly or indirectly from the use of this book. For legal or any other advice, please consult an experienced attorney or the appropriate expert, who is aware of the specific facts of your case and knows the law in your jurisdiction.

LaRosa & Associates
1225 King Street, Suite 802
Wilmington, DE 19801-3246
(302) 888-1290
www.LaRosaLaw.com

Testimonials

"You were an excellent choice for an attorney, someone who truly works hard for the working people of this state. Losing your job of many years is an emotional and stressful situation to go through. You made me feel I was not going through it by myself. You are definitely in the right line of work. God bless you and your family. Once again, thank you for taking my case personally."

– BW & TW

****

"If someone were in need of legal counsel, I would highly recommend John LaRosa. John is extremely detail oriented, and will leave "no stone unturned" when reviewing his clients' situations. He will also fight like a pit bull for what is right. I've been a client and a friend of John's for many years, and he exemplifies professionalism."

– NM

****

"John LaRosa represented me in an employment matter. He was professional, responsive and clearly discussed all the details and possible outcomes of my case. I highly recommend John."

– SB

****

"Mr. LaRosa was extremely knowledgeable and thorough throughout the entire process. He professionally assessed the strength of my case and successfully negotiated a settlement with my employer. I especially appreciated his honesty and ease of contact."

– TM

****

"I cannot even begin to express how I am feeling right now. You are an astonishing lawyer. It seemed at first things were looking bleak at the beginning, but with your expertise and persistence, the outcome was extraordinary. It was great!"

– LJ

****

TABLE OF CONTENTS

About The Author

For over 20 years, I've practiced plaintiff's employment law, although I call it "Employee Rights Law" because I exclusively represent employees in cases involving wrongful termination or other unlawful employment actions, such as denial of promotion, denial of hire, and harassment based on discrimination, retaliation, or other illegal reasons.

I am licensed in the States of Delaware, Pennsylvania, and New Jersey; the U.S. Court of Appeals for the Third Circuit sitting in Philadelphia; and the U.S. Supreme Court. I currently practice from my office in Wilmington, Delaware.

CHAPTER 1

DISCRIMINATION, COMPLAINTS, AND RETALIATION IN THE WORKPLACE

Discrimination in the workplace occurs when an employer takes an adverse employment action (e.g., termination, denial of promotion, demotion), or in some other way discriminates in the terms, conditions, or privileges of the employment of an employee compared to a similarly situated coworker because of a protected category such as race, color, national origin (birthplace, ethnicity, or ancestry), religion, sex (including pregnancy and sexual orientation), disability or perceived disability, or age (40 years old or older).

Typically, discrimination in the workplace financially impacts the employee against whom the employment action is taken, while a similarly situated employee outside of the protected category (or sufficiently younger by at least five years if the category is age) does not face the same type of action.

Employers will often claim to have had a legitimate non-discriminatory business reason for taking the action, but the employee and his attorney will assert that the legitimate non-discriminatory business reason is merely a pretext or an excuse for the adverse employment action that was taken. Upon closer examination, the "legitimate non-discriminatory" reason will not hold water - particularly where a similarly situated employee outside of the protected category (or at least five years younger) was treated differently under similar circumstances by the same decision-maker (i.e., the same supervisor, in most cases).

Workplace Harassment

Harassment in the workplace is typically characterized as severe or pervasive. If it does not happen on a daily basis, it happens on a weekly or otherwise very frequent basis. In many cases, workplace harassment is carried out because of sex, but unlawful harassment can be carried out because of any protected category (e.g., race, religion, disability) other than age.

For example, if a male boss constantly asks his female employee to go to dinner with him, subjects her to unwanted touching (e.g., shoulder rubs while she is at her desk), or makes sexual comments about her body, she would have solid grounds for bringing a valid harassment complaint to the human resources department.

Whistleblower Complaints

A whistleblower complaint is a complaint by an employee regarding a violation of federal, state, or local law that pertains to health, safety, or environmental hazards, a violation of an employer's rule, or a violation of a federal, state, or local law dealing with accounting mismanagement, fraud, deceit, or misappropriation of public or private funds by the employer. A whistleblower complaint is made by an employee to their supervisor, to someone else within the organization, or to a public body such as a federal agency, a law enforcement agency, or a legislator.

Employer Retaliation

Often, an employer retaliates against an employee as a result of the employee speaking up about something, such as a wrongdoing that the employer has not addressed (and may not want to address). For instance, an employer might retaliate against a government employee who reports misappropriation of public or private funds by his boss.

Employer retaliation also can occur in response to something as simple as reporting a state health code violation. For example, if an employer were to fire a kitchen employee for reporting a violation of the state health laws in the restaurant where he works, that could be unlawful employer retaliation.

As another example, if an employee reports sexual harassment to the human resources department or to the harasser's boss and asks for the employer to address the issue, the employer might terminate that employee's employment in an attempt to "shut them up" and get back to business as usual, rather than appropriately address the complaint.

From Subtle to Egregious: Forms of Employer Retaliation

Employer retaliation can be subtle or blatant. In some of the most egregious cases, an employee will be fired within a matter of days of raising an issue, such as discrimination. In more subtle cases, an employee who files a complaint, such as discrimination or whistleblowing, will be subject to a change in the terms, conditions, or privileges of employment. For example, the employee might be excluded from work emails or meetings or moved from a large office to a small cubicle. Retaliation even can be as subtle as not having a birthday party at work for an employee. While employees do not have a legal right to a birthday party, if an employer recognizes the birthdays of all of its employees in the same way except one employee (i.e., the employee who made a discrimination, harassment, or whistleblower complaint), the employer could rightfully be accused of retaliation.

A recent case of mine involved a police officer who experienced employer retaliation for filing a charge of discrimination. A retaliation case was brought against the police department based on the fact that the police officer's supervisor made it clear to the officer that he was giving a holiday gift to everyone in the unit except my client. In this case, the employer's retaliation took the form of a subtle microaggression. When occurring just once, such actions may not be legally significant, but the more often they occur, the more obvious the retaliation becomes, and the stronger the case of unlawful discrimination in the workplace becomes.

CHAPTER 2

AT-WILL EMPLOYMENT AND WRONGFUL TERMINATION

At-will employment is the legal doctrine that states that an employer can terminate an employee's employment at any time, with or without cause, and with or without advance notice. It also means that an employee can choose to quit or resign at any time, for any reason, with or without notice. Two weeks' notice is a courtesy that employers might expect, but in reality—absent a written contract—there usually is no legal obligation for an employee to provide two weeks' notice before resigning.

As an employee rights attorney, I deal with the exception to the at-will employment doctrine, which is that an employer can terminate the employment for any reason *as long as it is not for an illegal reason*, such as any form of discrimination prohibited by Title VII of the Civil Rights Act of 1964 ("Title VII"), the Americans with Disabilities Act ("ADA"), the Age Discrimination in Employment Act ("ADEA"), the Delaware Discrimination in Employment Act, the Delaware Persons with Disabilities Employment Protection Act ("DEPA"), the Delaware Whistleblowers' Protection Act, or the Delaware Workers' Compensation Improvement Act.

A specific example of wrongful termination (i.e., termination for an illegal reason) is age discrimination, which typically occurs when an employee who is age 40 or older is fired and replaced (by someone who is at least five years younger) because of their age.

I once handled a case that involved an employee who was in his early 60s and had just received his 40th anniversary gift from his corporate employer. Subsequently, he was assigned to a younger supervisor who was in their late 30s. My client received one performance improvement plan 40 years into his career stating that he needed to do a better job, and within 90 days, he was fired and replaced by someone sufficiently younger by at least five years. This happened despite the fact that before the performance improvement plan, the older employee had an unblemished record of virtually no discipline for over 40 years. This was a classic case of age discrimination.

Another example of wrongful termination is a termination that occurs as retaliation by an employer against a female employee who brings a sexual harassment complaint against her male boss to the human resources department.

Yet another example is an employee with a physical or mental limitation, who requests and is denied a reasonable accommodation to help him perform the essential functions of the job, and then is fired because of his disability.

Involuntary Termination of Employment

Involuntary termination can take the form of 1) an actual discharge through a firing for cause or a layoff or 2) a constructive discharge (i.e., forced resignation).

Actual Discharge: Firings and Layoffs

If the employer fires for cause, it means that the employer claims the firing is due to poor performance, unacceptable conduct, or attendance issues of the employee. In a layoff scenario, the employer usually claims that the employee's specific position is being eliminated or there is a mass reduction in force, meaning the jobs of more than one employee are being eliminated and that there is a non-discriminatory business reason for the layoff (e.g., budget cuts). It is important for an employee to try to obtain the employer's specific, stated reason for the termination of employment, at least verbally but preferably in writing.

Constructive Discharge

Another type of involuntary termination of employment that does not involve an actual firing or a layoff is a constructive discharge. In a constructive discharge case, the employee typically has quit without notice when the working conditions become so intolerable that the employee feels they have no other choice but to resign. Some prior situations that may indicate a constructive discharge eventually occurred include (1) a threat of being fired, (2) suggestions or encouragement to resign, (3) a demotion or a reduction of pay or benefits, (4) involuntary transfer to a less desirable position, (5) alteration of job responsibilities, (6) unsatisfactory job evaluations, and (7) false accusations of misconduct. All seven of these situations need not occur to establish a forced resignation, but the more of these situations that occurred before the employee left the job, the stronger the case of constructive discharge becomes.

Voluntary Termination or Voluntary Quit

In contrast to a constructive discharge, a voluntary termination of employment (also known as a voluntary quit) occurs when the employee freely decides to leave the company. A voluntary quit is typically characterized by a planned or written resignation (usually with advance notice), or by a situation where the employer offered to address the issue but the employee instead chose to leave the job, or by the employee's decision to obtain new employment elsewhere before making a planned exit from the company.

A *voluntary* termination is not a wrongful termination of employment. In a voluntary quit, the employee typically will not take legal action against the employer. In this scenario, it may be wise to provide two weeks' notice, particularly if the employee will want to use the employer as a positive job reference in the future.

Conversely, in an *involuntary* termination of employment, there is either a constructive discharge (i.e., forced resignation) or an actual discharge (e.g., firing, layoff). The employee will assert that the real reason the employment ended was an illegal reason such as discrimination or retaliation, and therefore, the discharge was a wrongful termination of employment.

CHAPTER 3

EMPLOYEE RIGHTS AND PROTECTIONS

Every employee has a right to file a complaint regarding employment discrimination or certain violations of the law. Such complaints of illegal action can be raised internally with the employer or externally with a governmental authority, such as the United States Equal Employment Opportunity Commission ("EEOC") or the Delaware Department of Labor. Such complaints are known as protected activity.

The employee also has a right to expect that the employer will address the issue and not discharge or retaliate against the employee for raising the very important issue in their protected activity.

When it comes to unlawful discrimination in the workplace, the law considers how an employee (current, former, or potential) who is claiming discrimination has been treated differently from similarly situated employees (current, former, or potential), typically by the same decision-maker. For example, if the same decision maker allows a male employee to miss a certain number of days with minor or no disciplinary measures, yet fires or issues harsher discipline to a female employee for having the same number of absences, then there may be grounds for a case of unlawful discrimination.

The EEOC and Mediation

The EEOC is the federal agency that handles charges of discrimination by employees (including current, former, and potential employees) if they allege discrimination on the basis of race, color, national origin (birthplace, ethnicity, or ancestry), sex (including pregnancy and sexual orientation), religion, disability or perceived disability, or age (40 or older).

The EEOC provides employees the opportunity to file a charge of discrimination against their employer and offers mediation to both the employee and employer. If the parties agree to mediate, then the EEOC will conduct a mediation in an attempt to resolve the employment dispute with a monetary remedy, a non-monetary remedy, or both.

Mediation typically is a one-day negotiation process where the employee can, with or without an attorney present, make a statement regarding the charge of discrimination. The employer, also with or without an attorney present, can respond to this statement. In most cases, the employer will respond through an attorney.

Rather than render a judgment as to which party is right and which is wrong (as a judge, a jury, or an arbitrator would do), the mediator's job is to facilitate the production of a negotiated settlement agreement between the parties by holding caucuses, which are private meetings between the mediator and one of the parties and their attorney. During these meetings, the parties make offers and counteroffers in an attempt to resolve the case with a monetary and/or a non-monetary resolution to the matter.

If the parties do not agree to mediate or if mediation is unsuccessful (i.e., the parties do not reach an agreement at mediation and the mediator declares an impasse or a deadlock), then the EEOC will forward the case to its Investigation Department and assign an investigator to the case. As part of the investigation, the employer will be given an opportunity to respond with a position statement with regard to the employee's charge of discrimination. In addition, the EEOC may conduct on-site interviews at the workplace or interview any witness whose name and phone number has been provided by the employee or the employer. The EEOC may also allow the employee to respond in writing to the employer's position statement. All of this is done in an attempt to determine whether unlawful discrimination indeed occurred as the employee alleges.

If the investigator concludes that discrimination indeed occurred, the EEOC can make a determination of cause in the employee's favor and then try to have the parties enter into a conciliation agreement to resolve the charge, with monetary and/or non-monetary remedies. Since the EEOC is not a court, it will not issue a court order or a judgment.

However, if the EEOC does not find cause for discrimination or if the parties do not enter into a conciliation agreement, the EEOC will issue a right to sue letter, which gives the employee 90 days from the date of receipt of that notice to file a lawsuit in federal or state court against the employer.

The requirement that employees exhaust their administrative remedy by filing a charge of discrimination with the EEOC (or the Delaware Department of Labor) and obtain a right to sue letter prior to filing with the court helps prevent federal and state courts from becoming overburdened with numerous employment cases. The EEOC and the Delaware Department of Labor also provide employees with a cheaper and faster way to resolve employment discrimination disputes than litigation in court.

The Delaware Discrimination in Employment Act

Employers must have at least 20 employees to be covered under federal age discrimination law and 15 employees to be covered by all other federal employment discrimination law and state disability discrimination law. However, the Delaware Discrimination in Employment Act ("DDEA") applies to employers with four or more employees in Delaware at the time of the discrimination. In addition to protecting employees against discrimination based on race, color, national origin (birthplace, ethnicity, ancestry), sex (including pregnancy and sexual orientation), religion, and age (40 or older), the DDEA prohibits employment discrimination based on additional protected categories including marital status, gender identity, and genetic information.

The Delaware Whistleblowers' Protection Act

The Delaware Whistleblowers' Protection Act prohibits employers from discharging or retaliating against an employee who reports a violation of federal, state, or local law dealing with health, safety, or environmental hazards, or violations of an employer rule or a federal, state, or local law dealing with financial mismanagement such as fraud, deceit, or misappropriation of public or private funds. This means that employees cannot be fired or discriminated against in the terms, conditions, location, or privileges of employment as a result of reporting such violations to their employer, a federal agency, a state legislator or a state legislative branch employee, a state or local elected official, or a law enforcement agency.

Contract Claims Under Delaware Law: Breach of Contract and Breach of the Covenant of Good Faith and Fair Dealing

In Delaware, an employee can pursue a common law claim for breach of contract, where there is a contract (such as a written employment agreement), the breach of an obligation imposed by that contract, and resulting damages to the employee.

In addition, with respect to the Delaware common law of contracts, there is something called the implied covenant of good faith and fair dealing. This covenant is an unwritten promise to deal with people in good faith and fairness in each contract made in Delaware, including each employment contract, including each employment relationship without a written contract.

A fired employee can bring a claim for breach of the covenant of good faith and fair dealing under four specific circumstances: (1) the termination violates public policy; (2) the employer misrepresents an important fact that the employee relied upon to accept a new position or remain in a present position; (3) the employer used its superior bargaining power to deprive the employee of clearly identifiable compensation related to the employee's past service, such as a sales commission; or (4) the employer falsified or manipulated employment records to create fictitious grounds for the termination of employment.

After the onset of the COVID-19 pandemic, I saw quite a few of the first variety of these claims (i.e., violation of a public policy by the employer). Early in the pandemic, I represented a client who was asked by his family doctor to quarantine for 14 days after his spouse was diagnosed with COVID-19. My client followed the quarantine request and tried to work from home during that time but was fired 12 days into his 14-day quarantine. In light of the Families First Coronavirus Response Act, which was based on federal public policies in favor of putting families first (before work) and slowing the spread of COVID-19, we were able to make the claim that the termination violated public policy.

That case was the perfect example of an employee who advanced public policies by heeding the direction of his doctor and staying home for 14 days, nursing his wife back to health, and protecting his employer and fellow employees from contracting COVID-19 from him. For these efforts, my client was discharged in retaliation. Thankfully, this case was successfully resolved in my client's favor.

The Delaware Workers' Compensation Improvement Act

Under the Delaware Workers' Compensation Improvement Act, it also is unlawful for an employer to fire or to retaliate against an employee because the employee claimed or attempted to claim workers' compensation benefits. Such an employee, who loses their position, may be restored to their employment or their position, privilege, right, or other condition of employment denied by the employer - unless they cease to be qualified to perform the duties of employment (as a result of the workplace injury). In addition, the employee may obtain lost compensation and damages (caused by the retaliation) as well as their costs and attorney's fees.

CHAPTER 4

RIGHTS AND REMEDIES FOR EMPLOYEES: A CLOSER LOOK

If an employee feels that their rights have been violated or that they are being treated unfairly in the workplace before or after filing a complaint against their employer, the employee may follow the company's internal complaint procedure. If satisfactory action is not taken by the employer, the employee should consult an employee rights attorney before taking legal action outside of the company.

However, at any point in the process—whether they are just considering or are still in the process of filing a complaint in accordance with the employer's internal complaint procedure—the employee has the right to consult an employee rights attorney.

Many companies have internal complaint procedures. If an employee has a complaint, particularly about harassment or discrimination, an employer's policy may expect the employee to report the issue directly to the harasser, then to the harasser's boss, and then to the human resources department. The employee should take whatever steps are included in the company's internal complaint procedure. However, if the employee is not comfortable confronting the harasser, which is often the case, they often will be permitted to initially report the harassment directly to the harasser's supervisor or to human resources.

In response to the complaint, the employer may conduct an investigation and reach a conclusion before the employee takes additional actions outside of the company. In some cases—particularly when the case involves union employees—the employer may have an alternative dispute resolution ("ADR") process or arbitration agreement. In this scenario, the employee may be required to undergo the ADR process, which could include mediation and/or arbitration.

Human Resources: To Trust or Not to Trust?

The simple fact of the matter is that a human resources representative is an employee of the company and usually sees his or her role as a guardian—one who is supposed to protect the company's legal interests whenever an employee reports an issue such as sexual harassment or other unlawful discrimination in the workplace.

Because human resources representatives are first and foremost representatives of the company, they are almost never advocates for an employee. For these reasons, an employee should not completely trust his company's human resources department. Instead, an employee who is facing such issues is well-advised to consult an employee rights attorney before bringing a complaint to human resources and before following through with the complaint beyond human resources.

Critical Time Limits for Taking Action

Charges of employment discrimination must be filed within 300 days (i.e., 42 weeks and six days, which is approximately 10 months) of the adverse action, such as termination. For example, if a former employee believes they were fired because of their national origin (birthplace, ethnicity, or ancestry), race, color, sex (including pregnancy and sexual orientation), religion, disability, perceived disability, or age (40 or older), then they need to file a charge of discrimination with the EEOC or the Delaware Department of Labor within 300 days of when they first learned that their employment would be terminated or was terminated.

Then, the employee must file a lawsuit in court within 90 days (i.e., 12 weeks and 6 days) of receiving their right to sue notice from the EEOC or the Delaware Department of Labor.

Other employment claims that do not involve a charge of discrimination may be filed directly in court as long as they are filed within the applicable statute of limitations. This time period could be as long as four years for a claim under Section 1981 of Title 42 of the U.S. Code (usually referred to simply as "Section 1981"), which deals with race discrimination in the making and enforcement of contracts. In Delaware, the statute of limitations is three years for a breach of contract, a breach of the covenant of good faith and fair dealing, or a retaliation claim under the Delaware Whistleblowers' Protection Act. Yet, the time limit is only two years for a claim under the Delaware Workers' Compensation Improvement Act or the federal Equal Pay Act which prohibits pay discrimination because of sex.

A former employee whose employment has been terminated or who believes that their employment rights have been violated should contact an employee rights attorney in order to ensure that they are aware of the time limits for filing their particular case.

Protections against Employer Retaliation

Federal and state laws prohibit employers from firing or retaliating against an employee who engages in the protected activity of filing a charge of discrimination, filing a lawsuit against the employer, or making an internal complaint of unlawful discrimination in the workplace, as well as participating in the investigation of or serving as a witness for an employee who has made a discrimination complaint (e.g., testifying as a witness on behalf of someone who claims sexual harassment).

Anyone who makes a complaint internally, to the EEOC, to the Delaware Department of Labor, or to a state or a federal court regarding discrimination because of race, color, national origin (birthplace, ethnicity, ancestry), sex (including pregnancy and sexual orientation), religion, disability, perceived disability, or age (40 or older), has legal protection under Title VII's opposition clause (or similar provisions in the ADA and the ADEA). There is similar legal protection for anyone who engages in a protected activity under the Delaware

Whistleblowers' Protection Act (e.g., reporting unlawful health, safety, or environmental hazards, or prohibited fraud, deceit, or misappropriation of public or private funds by the employer).

Each of these complaints is considered a legally "protected activity." This means that the employee would have additional legal protection by way of bringing a claim of retaliation against the employer should the employer take action against the employee for engaging in the legally protected activity.

What might start out as a minor complaint, (such as a female employee saying, "I don't like the sexual jokes that my male supervisor continues to make verbally and in emails, because a lot of them are sexist and I find them offensive,") could become more serious if the employer fails to address the issue and instead takes retaliatory action against the complaining employee (e.g., discipline, transfer, demotion, or firing of the employee). Under these circumstances, the employee would have a valid claim of retaliation against the employer.

The Right to Have an Attorney Present

An employee can request that an attorney be present for any conversation they have with the employer, but such a request typically would be governed by the nature of the employment. Union employees and some state government employees (i.e., state merit employees) have a right to have an attorney present during certain steps of an internal process. More often, however, an attorney is present only during more formal stages that allow the employee to grieve an employment dispute, such as an arbitration hearing.

In the private sector, where there is often only an informal, internal meeting to address a workplace dispute (including a complaint of sexual harassment or discrimination against a protected category), employers generally expect employees to discuss the issue with their boss and/or human resources, and there is no standalone right for the employee to have an attorney present in such meetings. However, the employee can contact an employee rights attorney for advice prior to or following such a meeting.

Courses of Action

There are several courses of action that an employee can take in response to employer retaliation and/or wrongful termination.

With an attorney, an employee may be able to send the employer a written demand letter seeking to informally resolve the employment dispute with a monetary remedy and/or a non-monetary remedy before the employee takes more formal legal action against the employer.

As previously discussed, an employee also can attempt to resolve an employment discrimination dispute with an employer on their own or with an attorney by filing a charge of discrimination with the EEOC or the Delaware Department of Labor.

Other employment disputes may be governed by an arbitration agreement that requires the employee to bring the claim to arbitration rather than to a judge or a jury in court. If the employee's employment is not governed by an arbitration agreement and the matter is not an employment discrimination dispute, then the employee could file a lawsuit in federal or state court immediately.

Depending on the circumstances, a case may be resolved through an arbitration hearing, a trial in court, or a mediation. Mediation can be carried out with a private mediator or as part of the process with the EEOC, the Delaware Department of Labor, the court, or the arbitration service provider, such as the American Arbitration Association.

In most cases, the best course of action is to first consult an employee rights attorney to determine whether the dispute merits taking action against the employer.

CHAPTER 5

IS IT WORTH IT TO SUE AN EMPLOYER?

As with many legal questions, the answer to this question is, "It depends on the specific facts and circumstances of the particular situation." In some cases, a discharged employee will be offered a severance package or a separation agreement in exchange for a signed promise not to pursue legal action against the employer. Under those circumstances, the employee should review the severance package or separation agreement with an employee rights attorney before accepting the agreement and signing away their legal rights.

In advising an employee about whether it is worth it to sue an employer, an employee rights attorney will consider many factors. One of the main factors is the viability of the case. Let's dig into this a bit deeper.

Viable Claim? Factors to Consider

When determining whether a claim of discrimination in the workplace is viable, I consider many factors in assessing the strengths and weaknesses of the employee's case as it relates to both 1) liability (whether the employer violated the law) and 2) damages (what monetary remedies could the employee recover for the employer's violation of the law).

Liability

1. **What is the Adverse Action?** Was the employee fired or laid off? Were multiple employees fired for the same incident? Were multiple employees laid off at the same time?

If there was no firing or layoff, was the employee forced to resign or retire due to intolerable working conditions that constitute a constructive discharge? Or did the employee voluntarily quit, give advance notice, and gracefully exit on their own volition. These questions are among the first to be answered.

2. **Does the stated reason by the employer hold water?** Is the employer's stated reason merely a pretext, excuse, fabrication, or disguise for the true reason—that true reason being discrimination or retaliation?

If the employee was fired for poor performance that was documented by a supervisor or fired for continued poor attendance after numerous instances of lateness or unexcused absence during their first six months of employment or fired for engaging in an altercation at work (regardless of whether they were the aggressor) and the employer fired both the employee and the aggressor, then the employer's stated reason may hold water, and the facts may not constitute a valid claim for discrimination or wrongful termination.

However, if there is an underlying, illegal reason, then I will further investigate whether the employee can meet their ultimate burden of showing that the employer's stated reason is false or that the real reason was more likely discrimination or retaliation.

3. Comparative treatment. How was the employee treated compared to similarly situated employees under similar circumstances? Was the employee fired for poor performance with no verbal or written warning after his co-worker received multiple write-ups and was retained? Was the employee fired after three instances of lateness while a co-worker was retained even though they were late to work four or more times? If the matter involved an altercation at the job site, was the employee fired while the employer retained the co-worker who was the aggressor? In all of these scenarios, was the co-worker a different race, sex, or age than the employee who was fired? Was there some other protected category that distinguishes the retained co-worker and the fired employee (e.g., disability status, religion, national origin)? Or did the employee engage in some protected activity that the retained co-worker did not?

4. Forms of Proof. Last, but perhaps most important, is the question of proving liability. Can it be proven that the employer acted illegally? To prove liability, it is very helpful to have witness testimony in writing (i.e., from signed witness statements, declarations, or affidavits) or from depositions. However, it is common for witnesses to be few and far between in these cases. Current and former employee witnesses might not want to testify on behalf of the employee (and thus against their current or former employer) for fear of risking their own career. Even if witnesses initially were willing to participate, sometimes their memories fade, or they are unable to be located because they have moved away or died.

The good news is that there are other ways to prove a case other than with witnesses - namely through documentation. E-mails, memos, a written termination letter, and/or the employee's performance record could help show wrongdoing on behalf of the employer. For instance, if the employee's performance record shows all or mostly satisfactory evaluations for several years until a new supervisor arrived who then soon replaced that employee with someone of a younger age or a different sex, that would raise questions, such as whether the new supervisor acted in a discriminatory way that contrasts with the employment record of the employee prior to the arrival of that supervisor.

Damages

5. What are the damages? How has the employee been harmed economically? If they were fired, are they still out of work, or are they now working a new job for less pay or fewer benefits?

If the employee was out of work for only a short period of time (e.g., three months) before obtaining a new, higher-paying job, then the termination actually might have been a blessing in disguise. Sometimes, when one door closes, another one opens. If the employee is enjoying greater financial opportunities, then they might not be suffering economic losses sufficient to justify spending the time and money necessary to pursue legal claim(s) against the employer.

However, the employee might have been fired for an illegal reason and is now making $20,000 per year less at a new job. On top of that, they may be suffering non-economic injuries such as injury to reputation, humiliation, embarrassment, and/or emotional distress. Regarding emotional distress, the employee may be experiencing major depression, anxiety disorder, or post-traumatic stress disorder because of the harassment or discrimination that they suffered from the prior employer. For these non-economic injuries, (which are not precisely calculable like economic losses), remedies called compensatory damages are available, particularly in cases brought under Title VII, the ADA, the DDEA, the DEPA, the Delaware Whistleblowers' Protection Act, and the Delaware Workers' Compensation Improvement Act.

6. **Did the employee fulfill their duty to mitigate their damages?** Ultimately, the employer has the burden of proving that the employee failed to mitigate or lessen their damages. However, the employee's duty to mitigate damages must also be considered by the employee and the employee's attorney. In any personal injury case, the plaintiff has a duty to mitigate their damages (such as by seeking medical treatment for a

broken arm sustained in an auto accident). Similarly, in an employment case, an employee is expected to take steps to mitigate or lessen their pain and suffering and their economic losses.

In employment cases, this can mean different things depending on the situation. In the context of wrongful termination, the employee usually must try to mitigate their damages by looking for substantially equivalent work in the same geographic area. For example, an employee who is fired from a bank in Wilmington, does not need to apply for banking jobs in California, and also does not need to accept the first fast food job that opens up in Wilmington. However, they do need to look for substantially equivalent work in the same geographic area, such as similar positions in the banking and financial industry in New Castle County, Delaware.

Employees who do not begin a new job search after being fired because they have unrelated health issues, or choose to resume their education and become a full-time student, or simply decide to retire early will have difficulty pursuing a wrongful termination case against their last employer. The employer can argue that the employee has failed to mitigate their economic losses. As a result, a jury or a judge can determine the employee is not entitled to an award of damages or only is entitled to a reduced award based on their failure to mitigate their damages.

CHAPTER 6

MORE THINGS TO CONSIDER: TIME, MONEY, AND FUTURE POSSIBILITIES

Pursuing a workplace discrimination case can be costly in terms of both time and money. Just how costly is not easy to determine until after consulting an employee rights attorney.

The employee also should consider their future career goals. For example, if the employee feels as though they have been forced to resign from a global corporation but would like to have the option to reapply to that same company or its subsidiaries in the future, then they might not want to bring a legal claim against that employer. This is because resolution of an employment dispute, if it is reached by a settlement, almost always will require the employee to promise not to reapply to the company in the future.

If an employee has not suffered significant economic losses or any emotional distress and was able to obtain substantially equivalent work or even higher-paying work in a short period of time (e.g., three months), then it might not be worth it for the employee to sue their former employer.

Remedies for Workplace Discrimination

If an employee successfully pursues a workplace discrimination case against their employer, they may recover damages and other remedies, including the following:

1. Back pay and benefits from the date of termination through the date of any trial verdict;

2. Either reinstatement of employment or front pay and benefits for a reasonable period of time from the date of the trial verdict going forward into the future;
3. Compensatory damages for emotional distress, humiliation, embarrassment, and injury to reputation, the value of which is more speculative than the aforementioned economic losses of back pay and benefits;
4. Reimbursement of the employee's attorney's fees and costs spent in resolving the case;
5. Punitive damages where the employer acted with malice or with reckless indifference to the employer's rights in a case brought under Title VII, the ADA, the DDEA, or the DEPA.
   a. Liquidated damages, which is a doubling of the compensatory damages, where the violation was willful in an ADEA case.

It should be noted that there is a statutory cap or limit on compensatory and punitive damages for Title VII, ADA, DDEA, and DEPA cases. This limit is based on the employer's number of employees. For employers with four to 100 employees, the compensatory damages and punitive damages are limited to just $50,000; for employers with 101 to 200 employees, the statutory cap is $100,000; for employers with 201 to 500 employees, the cap is $200,000; and for employers with over 500 employees, the cap is $300,000.

In a typical employment discrimination case against an employer with over 500 employees, the maximum recovery for an employee who wins at trial would be 100% of their back pay and benefits from the date of termination to the date of trial plus $300,000 for compensatory and punitive damages plus reimbursement of their attorney's fees and costs. In addition, reinstatement or front pay could be awarded.

If the case is resolved through settlement, the employee agrees to accept a sum that is almost always less than the maximum recovery that could have been awarded at a trial (or an arbitration hearing). However, additional remedies sometimes can be obtained such as a letter of reference for the employee and outplacement services that assist the employee in obtaining another job.

Remedies Typically <u>Not</u> Available

It is unrealistic for an employee to expect these remedies as part of an employment settlement:

- Admission of wrongdoing by the employer. Most employment settlement agreements will state that the settlement is not an admission of guilt, fault, or wrongdoing by the company.
- An apology from the employer, no matter how egregious the termination. Over the course of my career, I have seen only a very few written apologies provided by an employer in the context of employment settlements.

In all cases, it is best for the individual to consult an experienced employee rights attorney who can evaluate the specific facts and circumstances of the termination or the employment dispute and advise the employee as to whether or not it makes sense to sue or take other legal action against the employer.

CHAPTER 7

HIRING AN EMPLOYEE RIGHTS ATTORNEY: WHEN, WHY, AND WHAT TO EXPECT

Some people hesitate to hire an employee rights attorney, even if they believe they have a strong case of workplace discrimination or wrongful termination. Often, the hesitation comes from the uncertainty of what to expect as well as an incomplete understanding of the value of an attorney in handling these types of cases.

Let's briefly explore the basics – the when, what, and why of hiring an employee rights attorney.

When to Hire an Employee Rights Attorney

To put it simply, sooner is always better than later, as there are steps that an employee can take very early on to protect and preserve the employee's rights and even strengthen their legal claims. An individual should contact an employee rights attorney as soon as they feel they have an employment dispute based on workplace discrimination or retaliation.

That said, an employee rights attorney can assist an employee at any point in the process of bringing a wrongful termination case or other claim. It is beneficial to involve an attorney even if the employee already has made an internal discrimination complaint with the employer or has filed a charge of discrimination on their own with the EEOC or the Delaware Department of Labor.

I certainly consult with employees who already have filed a charge and received a right to sue letter, assuming the right to sue letter has not yet expired. I also represent employees who already have filed a lawsuit but need an employee rights attorney to pursue the case in court.

What to Expect

During the first conversation with an employee rights attorney, an employee can expect to provide some basic information, such as the name of the employer, the type of job and job title they held or currently hold with the employer, the number of years they have worked for the employer, the employer's stated reason for the termination or adverse employment action, and why the employee thinks that that action was unfair or illegal.

Next, the employee can expect to be asked to provide some documents to the attorney, such as a resumé, a job description, an employee handbook, performance reviews, disciplinary action, a termination notice, W-2s or tax returns for the prior three years at the job in question, a summary or description of the employee benefits plan, the personnel file (if the employee has access to it), the separation agreement (when offered), and any other documents that the employee thinks might be relevant to the case.

What to Look For

There are several things a person should look for in an employee rights attorney, including:

- **Area of expertise.** Does the attorney focus exclusively on employment law, or does the attorney dabble in employment law and other areas such as personal injury, business law, or criminal defense? It is preferable to choose an attorney who focuses exclusively on employment law. It also is important to keep in mind that an employee who represents both employers and employees in such disputes may be less sympathetic to the employee than an employee rights attorney who exclusively represents employees.
- **Length of time in practice.** Has the attorney been practicing employee rights law for multiple decades, or are they new to the representation of employees, new to the practice of employment law, or new to the practice of law in general?

- **State(s) of licensure.** Is the attorney licensed to practice in the state where the employment claim arose? For example, if a person was working in Delaware, they should look to hire an attorney who is licensed in the State of Delaware, even if the employee lives in Pennsylvania, New Jersey, or another state. Conversely, if a person was working in Pennsylvania, they should hire an attorney who is licensed in Pennsylvania even if the employee lives outside of Pennsylvania. If a person was working in New Jersey, they should hire an attorney who is licensed in New Jersey even if the employee lives outside of New Jersey.

Why Hire an Attorney?

An employee rights attorney is the best person to advise someone in terms of how to handle ongoing harassment or discrimination, and/or gracefully exit the company with one's legal rights and professional reputation intact. An employee rights attorney also can help an employee avoid costly mistakes that could delay progress in or harm the viability of their case.

LaRosa & Associates: Delaware's Longest Continuously Operating Law Firm Dedicated Exclusively to Employee Rights

In contrast to other law firms, LaRosa & Associates in Delaware represents employees exclusively - not defendant employers. We also focus exclusively on employee rights law, which means we do not divide our time between multiple practice areas (e.g., personal injury, business law) like other firms. Individuals who contact LaRosa & Associates receive personalized attention and service from an employee rights attorney and will not have to worry about their case being delegated to junior lawyers or non-attorney staff.

To my knowledge, no one in Delaware has practiced employee rights law *exclusively* longer than I have. Because this is the only area of the law in which I practice, I am highly specialized, completely focused, and extremely dedicated to employee rights. I am truly passionate about this area of practice. It has been my life's work for over 20 years now. I have been fortunate enough to champion the rights of hundreds of employees in and near Delaware. This fight for justice in the workplace continues to this day.

APPENDIX

REPRESENTATIVE CASES

I. LARGE RECOVERIES

A. *Age Discrimination.* Obtained a six-figure settlement for a 62-year-old Demand Planner employed by a global chemical company for 40 years who was placed on a six-month performance improvement plan and fired five months later, allegedly for inability to meet job standards, by his 35-year-old manager who replaced him with a 28-year-old employee (EEOC).

B. *Racial Harassment; Retaliation; Unpaid Leave.* Obtained a six-figure settlement for an African-American Director placed on unpaid leave from a global pharmaceutical company after she reported racial harassment in the workplace by her Caucasian supervisors (Del. Dep't of Labor).

C. *Sex Discrimination; Hostile Work Environment Because of Sex; Retaliation.* Obtained a six-figure settlement plus 20 weeks of COBRA benefits for a female General Manager of two sites for a waste management company who after earning a pay raise, stock grants, and 100% of her performance-based bonus, was harassed by her new, male supervisor; reported his discriminatory treatment to human resources; and then was fired and replaced by her male peer who previously was entrusted to manage only one site (Out-of-Court Settlement).

D. *Sexual Harassment; National Origin and Religious Discrimination; Retaliation.* Obtained a six-figure settlement for an award-winning, Indian, female, Hindu, Ph.D. Chemical Engineer for a global chemical company who was discriminated against and fired due to her internal complaints of sex, ethnic, and religious discrimination (Am. Arb. Ass'n).

E. *Genetic Information and Disability Discrimination.* Obtained a settlement for a Software Consultant discharged over the telephone just seven days after he informed his manager by e-mail that he just had a cancerous tumor removed from his bladder and would need additional outpatient treatments before work for six weeks (D. Minn.).

F. *Sexual Orientation Discrimination.* Obtained a six-figure contract buyout for a homosexual Public School Principal whose contract was non-renewed because of her sexual orientation (Del. Dep't of Labor).

G. *Reverse Race Discrimination; Age Discrimination; Contract Non-renewal.* Obtained a six-figure recovery for a then 55-year-old, Caucasian Public School Principal whose contract was non-renewed by her African-American Superintendent who previously stated publicly that she wanted more "African Americans" and more "young people" in leadership roles (D. Del.).

H. *Delaware Whistle Blowers' Protection Act.* Obtained a $300,000 settlement for a Town Manager fired for reporting the Treasurer's mismanagement of public funds, the Police Chief's misappropriation of public resources, and nonresident developers' acts against the public interest (Del. Super., Kent Cty).

I. *Delaware Workers' Compensation Improvement Act; Breach of the Covenant of Good Faith and Fair Dealing.* Obtained a six-figure settlement for an HVAC Technician laid off just 11 days after returning from workers' compensation leave and five months after his leave to care for his son whose school was closed for reasons related to COVID-19 (Out-of-Court Settlement).

J. *Breach of Contract; Shareholders' Agreement; Executive Compensation; Arbitration.* Obtained a six-figure structured settlement for a retired President and minority shareholder of a medical practice who expanded the practice from six to eight locations and increased the business's revenue. Upon retirement, the client was denied payment for his shares of stock and two annual bonuses and was sued by his former employer. All claims against him were dismissed as part of the settlement obtained on his behalf (Del. Ch.).

K. *Wage Payment and Collection Act; Merger; Breach of the Covenant of Good Faith and Fair Dealing; Breach of Contract.* Assisted as local counsel in obtaining a six-figure settlement for the President of a software sales start-up company who was wrongfully discharged by its CEO to avoid paying him a retention bonus and other earned compensation after the employer merged with a competitor (Del. Super.).

L. *WARN Act Violations; Mass Layoff, Plant Closings.* Assisted as local Delaware counsel in procuring a large settlement of a class action brought by 45 named employees on behalf of a class of over 250 workers subject to a mass layoff who were not provided sufficient advance written notice of the terminations of their employment as required by federal law (Bankr. D. Del.).

M. *Age Discrimination; Termination of Employment.* Obtained a six-figure recovery for a 60-year-old Railroad Engineer fired by his 28-year-old General Manager after refusing to commute nearly three hours to a job (E.D. Pa.).

N. *Government Discrimination; Race Discrimination in Contracts.* Obtained a six-figure recovery for an African-American President of a business denied a contract with a state college because of his race (D. Del.).

O. *Severance; Negotiation.* Negotiated a severance package of more than 20 months' base salary worth in excess of half of a million dollars for the President of a healthcare insurance company without asserting any legal claims (Out-of-Court Settlement).

II. TRIAL VERDICTS, COURT JUDGMENTS & AWARDS

A. *Breach of Contract; Quantum Meruit.* Won a verdict in the trial of an Accountant whose longtime employer failed to deduct his social security and Medicare taxes for five years and then sued him after it had to pay the IRS on his behalf. Judgment was entered for the employee, and all claims against him were dismissed (Del. Com. Pl., New Castle Cty).

B. *Breach of Contract; Promissory Note.* Won a verdict in the trial for a woman who made a loan pursuant to a promissory note to two home construction contractors and their partnership (Del. Com. Pl., New Castle Cty).

C. *Police Chief Due Process.* Won immediate reinstatement after a five-day hearing for a Police Chief charged with 17 counts of alleged misconduct and suspended for over five months. All charges were dismissed, and the client returned to work (Sussex Cty, Del.).

D. *First Amendment Freedom of Speech and Right to Petition for Redress of Grievances.* Obtained a judgment for a Police Lieutenant denied three promotions to Captain despite ranking first on the promotion test after he testified before a federal grand jury against the County Executive and his Chief Administrative Officer (D. Del.).

E. *Breach of Employment Contract.* Defeated town's appeal of its previously denied motion to dismiss the breach of employment contract claim of a Town Manager fired less than ten months into his five-year contract (Del. Supr.).

F. *Arbitration; Benefits Under a Collective Bargaining Agreement.* Sustained a grievance restoring all vacation and sick leave and compensating for missed shift differential, holiday pay, and acting Sergeant's pay to a Police Officer who, despite being cleared for duty by his cardiologist, was not permitted to work for allegedly non-work-related chest pain sustained after chasing a suspected drug dealer on foot (Am. Arb. Ass'n).

III. AGE DISCRIMINATION

A. *Retaliation; Age Discrimination; Termination of Employment.* Negotiated a settlement and health benefits for one year for a 55-year-old Marketing Director of a Fortune 500 company who was fired less than six weeks after he filed a charge of age discrimination against its President who is 15 years younger than him (EEOC).

B. *Age Discrimination; Forced Resignation.* Obtained a settlement for a 58-year-old Director of a global chemical company who was told he would be fired if he did not retire (EEOC).

C. *Age Discrimination; Sex Discrimination; Unpaid Administrative Leave; Performance Improvement Plan.* Obtained a settlement for an award-winning, 50-year-old, female Director of a healthcare system arising from her younger, male supervisor's placement of her on a five-month performance improvement plan ("PIP"), placement of her on unpaid administrative leave, and discharge of her less than four months after issuing her the five-month PIP (D. Del.).

D. *Demotion; Age Discrimination; Constructive Discharge.* Obtained a settlement for a 67-year-old Trademark Paralegal of a Fortune 500 apparel company who was demoted with a reduction in pay and forced to resign because of her age (EEOC).

IV. DISABILITY DISCRIMINATION

A. *Disability Discrimination; Age Discrimination.* Obtained a settlement for a 53-year-old Department Store Manager who was fired by her younger District Manager four months after she informed her that she had severe arthritis in her hip (EEOC).

B. *Disability Discrimination; History of Impairment; Involuntary Leave of Absence.* Obtained a monetary settlement plus medical and dental benefits for one year for a CDL-licensed Truck Driver employed by a liquor distributor for over 34 years who was not allowed to return to work after suffering a single, unprovoked seizure despite obtaining clearance from his doctor and waivers from the state and the federal departments of transportation (Del. Dep't of Labor).

C. *Perceived Disability and Age Discrimination; Delaware Workers' Compensation Improvement Act.* Obtained a settlement for an EMT/Firefighter who was forced to undergo a fitness for duty test, suspended just nine months after filing a workers' compensation claim for a knee injury, and encouraged to resign by the President of the fire company who said, "Let's face it. You are 45." (EEOC).

D. *Involuntary Layoff; Perceived Disability Discrimination.* Obtained a settlement for a Sales Assistant for a global financial services firm who was laid off less than a month after she disclosed the fact that she might have bipolar disorder (EEOC).

E. *Disability Discrimination; Termination of Employment.* Obtained a settlement on behalf of a 68-year-old Receptionist wrongfully suspended and eventually terminated one day after disclosing to her General Manager that she was a leukemia survivor (EEOC).

F. *Retaliation; Perceived Disability Discrimination; Termination of Employment.* Obtained a settlement for a Purchasing Agent of a textile company who was fired two days after she complained to human resources that her manager's bullying caused her to have panic attacks (EEOC).

G. *Due Process and Government Discrimination Under the Fourteenth Amendment and 42 U.S.C. § 1983; Delaware Handicapped Persons Employment Protection Act.* Obtained a settlement for a municipal office employee with a prescription for medical marijuana for her Lyme Disease who was refused a reasonable accommodation; administered a drug test; denied in violation of the town's drug and alcohol policy a retest which was provided to her non-disabled, male co-worker; and ultimately discharged (Del. Dep't of Labor).

V. WHISTLE BLOWING & RETALIATION

A. *Delaware Whistle Blowers' Protection Act; Contract Non-renewal.* Obtained a settlement for the Cafeteria Manager of a state school district whose contract was non-renewed after he reported to the state department of education and the U.S. Department of Agriculture that a Building Principal misappropriated school funds (Del. Super.).

B. *Delaware Whistle Blowers' Protection Act and Sex and Age Discrimination.* Obtained a settlement for a 47-year-old female Store Manager of a national pharmacy chain who was fired less than four months after she internally reported a younger, male Vice President after he unsuccessfully tried to flirt with her, made ageist comments about her age, and physically grabbed her (D. Del.).

C. *Pay Disparity; Age Discrimination; Delaware Whistle Blowers' Protection Act.* Obtained a settlement for a Nursing Home Dietician who was paid less than her younger peers and then discharged after she responded to a survey by the state department of health that resulted in the employer receiving deficiencies from the state and the federal governments (D. Del.).

D. *Breach of the Covenant of Good Faith and Fair Dealing; Delaware Whistle Blowers' Protection Act.* Obtained a settlement for a Vice President and Bank Branch Manager who was discharged after reporting to human resources her Regional Manager's improper transfer of loans and falsification of related records in violation of federal and state law and the bank's code of ethics (D. Del.).

E. *Delaware Workers' Compensation Improvement Act; Constructive Discharge (Forced Resignation).* Obtained a settlement for a Pharmacist who claimed workers' compensation benefits for bilateral carpal tunnel syndrome and was forced to resign after he was denied an effective accommodation, issued a written warning for an incident that occurred eight months earlier, harassed with text messages on his days off, threatened with discharge, encouraged to resign, falsely accused of misconduct, and issued a level 2 reprimand for a first offense in violation of the employer's custom or practice (Del. Super., Sussex Cty).

F. *Delaware Whistleblowers' Protection Act; Breach of the Covenant of Good Faith and Fair Dealing.* Obtained a settlement for a Business Systems Analyst discharged during the COVID-19 pandemic by a newspaper publisher less than one month after he reported to the state division of public health that his employer had no COVID-19 plan in place and its employees were permitted to remove their masks indoors (Out-of-Court Settlement).

G. *Delaware Workers' Compensation Improvement Act; Retaliation; Layoff.* Obtained a settlement for a Secretary employed by a beer distributor for over 21 years who was laid off just five days after she reported to its Human Resources Director that she had carpal tunnel syndrome (Del. Super., New Castle Cty).

H. Retaliation; Race Discrimination; 42 U.S.C. § 1981; Title VII. Obtained a settlement for an African-American Senior Operations Engineer employed by a global chemical company for 17 years who was discharged by a Caucasian just eight months after he became his manager and just two months after the client reported to human resources race discrimination by his Caucasian peer who twice called an African-American Technician, "boy." (EEOC).

I. Retaliation and Race Discrimination; Demotion. Obtained a settlement package with a contract buyout for an African-American Public School Administrator who was demoted just two days after she reported to human resources a hostile work environment because of her race (EEOC).

VI. SEX & PREGNANCY DISCRIMINATION

A. *Quid Pro Quo Sexual Harassment; Pregnancy Discrimination; Retaliation; Reduction in Force.* Obtained a settlement for a female Lab Technician whose job was eliminated as part of an alleged reduction in force by the married male Executive Director of a global research and development organization after he impregnated her and she returned from pregnancy leave and ended his affair with her (EEOC).

B. *Pregnancy and Disability Discrimination; Reduction in Pay and Forced Resignation.* Obtained a settlement for a Senior Registered Client Service Associate of a Fortune 100 company who was forced to resign after a reduction in her pay and a transfer from a desk to a cubicle shortly after she returned from disability and maternity leaves after a difficult pregnancy (EEOC).

C. *Pregnancy Discrimination; Demotion.*

Obtained a settlement for a female Chief Financial Officer of a textile company who was demoted while on pregnancy leave (EEOC).

D. *Pregnancy and Race Discrimination; Retaliation.*

Obtained severance pay for an African-American, surrogate mother employed by a state university as its Director of Student Affairs and Engagement who disclosed her pregnancy, was harassed, reported pregnancy discrimination, and was disciplined after she took pregnancy leave and returned to work (EEOC).

E. *Severance; Retaliation; Sex Discrimination.*

Negotiated a severance package for a bank's female Senior Vice President discharged after informing the CEO he was running an "all boys' club." (Out-of-Court Settlement).

F. *Quid Pro Quo Sexual Harassment; Retaliation; Unpaid Suspension.* Obtained a settlement for a female Account Manager of a collection agency who was placed on unpaid suspension after she reported to human resources that its male CEO sexually harassed her by verbally propositioning her for sex in exchange for more pay and texting shirtless photos of himself to her cell phone (Out-of-Court Settlement).

G. *Hostile Work Environment; Symbolic Harassment; Racial and Sexual Harassment; Retaliation.* Obtained a settlement for an African-American female Mortgage Underwriter who after twice complaining about black dildos being placed on her desk, was demoted, transferred to another state with no compensation for the increased commute and travel expenses, and forced to resign (D. Del.).

H. *Sexual Harassment; Retaliation; Discharge.* Obtained a settlement for a 28-year-old female Paralegal who was discharged just five months after she reported physical and verbal sexual harassment in the workplace by her male supervisor (EEOC).

I. *Sex Discrimination; Assault and Battery.*

Obtained a settlement for a female employee of an international food distributor who was the victim of a physical assault and battery in the workplace by her female supervisor who was not discharged or disciplined for this illegal conduct because the supervisor was sexually involved with a male manager (D. Del.).

VII. RACE & ETHNIC DISCRIMINATION

A. Race Discrimination; Age Discrimination.

Obtained a settlement for a 61-year-old, African-American Fraud Investigator of a bank who was discharged by her younger, Caucasian supervisor for allegedly poor performance after the client received numerous awards during her more than 30 years of service (EEOC).

B. Race Discrimination; Age Discrimination; Demotion; Constructive Discharge. Obtained a settlement for a 49-year-old African-American Director of Rehabilitation of a skilled nursing facility who received all positive evaluations and no prior written criticism but was forced to resign when she was demoted to an unspecified, non-management position with less pay and replaced by a younger, Caucasian Director whose prior facility ended its contract with the employer (EEOC).

C. *Race Discrimination; Constructive Discharge.* Obtained a settlement for an African-American oil refinery worker who was wrongfully blamed for two workplace accidents, improperly drug tested, and ultimately forced to retire prematurely after more than 25 years of service (E.D. Pa.).

D. *Denials of Promotions; Constructive Discharge; Retaliation; Race and Color Discrimination; Pregnancy Discrimination.* Obtained a settlement for a pregnant, black, African-American Accountant with a Master's Degree forced to resign after she was denied two promotions to the unposted positions of 1) Controller given to a less experienced, non-pregnant, Caucasian female with no college degree who the Human Resources Manager admitted was not qualified for the position and 2) Accounts Payable and Purchasing Manager given to a Caucasian male after he threatened to resign from the company (EEOC).

E. *Constructive Discharge; Sexual Harassment; National Origin Discrimination.* Obtained a settlement for a Hispanic female Leasing Assistant of an apartment management company who was forced to resign after being physically and verbally sexually harassed for four months and then criticized for her "Puerto Rican attitude" by the company's President (EEOC).

F. *National Origin Discrimination; Ethnic Harassment; Retaliation.* Negotiated a severance of salary and health benefits for seven months for an immigrant Operations Manager of a real estate company who reported ethnic discrimination to human resources after her supervisor mocked her foreign accent (EEOC).

G. *Termination of Employment; Race Discrimination.* Obtained a settlement for an African-American employee of a food processing plant discharged for failure to return after injuring his shoulder on the job (D. Del.).

H. *Race Discrimination; Religious Discrimination.* Obtained a settlement for an African-American, Muslim Forklift Operator discharged by a food service distributor for calling out of work once with proper advance notice due to a death in his immediate family after his Caucasian, Christian peer was retained despite previously that same month calling out for Mother's Day (Out-of-Court Settlement).

I. *Race Discrimination in State Government Employment.* Won a Motion to Amend a Complaint to include claims of racial discrimination under the federal civil rights laws against racial (42 *U.S.C.* § 1981) and governmental discrimination (42 *U.S.C.* § 1983) on behalf of an African-American Nurse wrongfully terminated by a state hospital (Del. Super., New Castle Cty).

VIII. SEXUAL ORIENTATION DISCRIMINATION

A. *Constructive Discharge; Sexual Orientation and Sex Discrimination; Retaliation.* Obtained a settlement for a homosexual, female Chef/Manager who was harassed, suspended, and forced to resign because of her sexual orientation and her sex and in retaliation for her complaints of unlawful workplace discrimination based on her sexual orientation and her sex (D. Del.).

B. *Sexual Orientation Discrimination; Denial of Promotion.* Obtained a promotion for a homosexual Biochemist previously denied multiple times in favor of less senior, heterosexual peers despite the fact that she received excellent performance evaluations and recommendations from her direct supervisor and his boss (Del. Dep't of Labor).

IX. REVERSE DISCRIMINATION

A. *Reverse Sex Discrimination; Termination of Employment.* Won an EEOC determination of cause for discrimination for a male Registered Nurse who was discharged by his female supervisors for sending a profane text message to a female peer who also sent him a profane text message but was not fired (EEOC).

B. *Reverse Sex Discrimination; Age Discrimination.* Obtained a settlement for a 57-year-old male employed by a manufacturer for over 38 years who was discharged and replaced by his younger supervisor's mistress (EEOC).

C. *Reverse Pregnancy Discrimination; Reverse Sex Discrimination; FMLA Retaliation.* Obtained a settlement for the male Assistant Vice President of a Fortune 100 bank who was falsely accused of misconduct and discharged by his female supervisor with no young children on the day he returned from paternity leave under the Family and Medical Leave Act ("FMLA") (EEOC).

X. FAMILY & MEDICAL LEAVE ACT

A. *FMLA Interference; Race Discrimination.* Obtained a settlement for an African-American Billing Coordinator for a medical practice who was discharged allegedly for being a no call, no show after she was required to return from telework to the office during the COVID-19 pandemic, was exposed to co-workers who did not wear masks as mandated, developed an upper respiratory infection, and was hospitalized but before she obtained medical clearance from her physician to again return to work (Out-of-Court Settlement).

B. *Breach of the Covenant of Good Faith and Fair Dealing; FMLA Retaliation; Perceived Disability Discrimination.* Obtained a settlement for the Director of a Billing and Collection company who was owed a large commission on a multi-million-dollar contract and was discharged five days after informing his boss he would need time off for shoulder surgery (Out-of-Court Settlement).

C. *Family and Medical Leave Act; Intermittent FMLA Leave; Interference; Discharge.* Obtained a settlement for the Premium Analyst of an insurance company who was issued a final written warning for overuse of FMLA time, retroactively denied intermittent medical leave two days after she used it, and then discharged the same day (Out-of-Court Settlement).

XI. BREACH OF CONTRACT & COVENANT OF GOOD FAITH & FAIR DEALING

A. *Breach of the Covenant of Good Faith and Fair Dealing; Breach of Contract.* Obtained a settlement for a Senior Director of Operations fired by the CEO of a technology start-up 10 days after he disclosed his wife's COVID-19 symptoms and his potential exposure to the virus and opted to self-quarantine and work from home for two weeks to slow the spread of the fatal disease and place the health of his family first (Am. Arb. Ass'n).

B. *Breach of Contract; Breach of the Covenant of Good Faith and Fair Dealing.* Obtained a settlement for a Director lured from his prior Vice President role and then fired for alleged non-performance just nine months into his employment contract containing broken promises of corporate objectives for his role, long-term share incentive plan participation, and six months' severance for any termination without cause (Out-of-Court Settlement).

XII. DENIALS OF PROMOTION & HIRING

A. *National Origin and Race Discrimination; Denial of Promotions in Local Government Employment.* Obtained a $215,000 settlement on behalf of two Hispanic Police Officers each denied promotion to Sergeant because of their ethnicity (D. Del.).

B. *Procedural Due Process Under the Fourteenth Amendment and 42 U.S.C. § 1983; Denial of Promotion.* Obtained a six-figure recovery on behalf of three longtime Police Sergeants each denied promotion to Lieutenant in favor of two less experienced officers including a Corporal in violation of state law requiring that Lieutenant promotees have at least two years' time in grade as Sergeants (D. Del.).

C. *Denial of Promotion; Retaliation; Involuntary Transfer; Sex and Age Discrimination.* Won an EEOC determination of cause for discrimination and eventually obtained a settlement for a 48-year-old female Director denied a promotion and involuntarily transferred to another department after she complained of sex and age discrimination by her younger male manager (EEOC).

D. *Pregnancy Discrimination; Denial of Promotion; Demotion.* Obtained a settlement for an Assistant Principal Intern who was denied promotion to Assistant Principal and demoted to Teacher just one month after she disclosed her pregnancy to the school district that then promoted a less qualified, non-pregnant Teacher to the Assistant Principal role who the Intern previously prevailed over for the internship (D. Del.).

E. *Race Discrimination; Denial of Promotion; Retaliation.* Obtained a settlement for an African-American Special Education Teacher who was twice denied a promotion that was first given to an unqualified Caucasian with whom the school district had preliminary conversations about the position before posting it and that was later re-titled and given to a second Caucasian after the Teacher filed a race discrimination complaint (D. Del.).

F. *Denial of Hire in State Government Employment; Race Discrimination.* Obtained a settlement for an African-American job applicant with a Master's Degree denied hire in favor of a Caucasian high school graduate who did not meet the minimum qualifications of the job (EEOC).

XIII. C-SUITE EXECUTIVES, ADMINISTRATORS & OTHER PROFESSIONALS

A. *Negotiation.* Represented the President, CEO, and sole stockholder of a local health insurance company in negotiating both 1) his sale of the corporation and its assets to a regional health insurance company for over four million dollars and 2) his multi-year employment contract as the President of a subsidiary of the purchasing company (Out-of-Court Settlement).

B. *Termination of Services of Professional Employees of a Public School District.* Negotiated the retirement of the longtime Superintendent of a successful, public school district who was falsely accused of immorality, misconduct in office, neglect of duty, and incompetence (Sussex Cty, Del.).

C. *Fourteenth Amendment Right to Privacy and First Amendment Rights of Association and Speech and Right to Petition the Government for Redress of Grievances.* Obtained a settlement for an Attorney whose constitutional right to privacy was violated when his confidential medical information was released to the news media by local government officials in retaliation for exercising his First Amendment rights to associate with his clients and speak out against the public officials' illegal actions (D. Del.).

INDEX

D

E

F

G

P

Q

R

V

W

NOTES

Made in United States
North Haven, CT
13 November 2026

22102018R00062